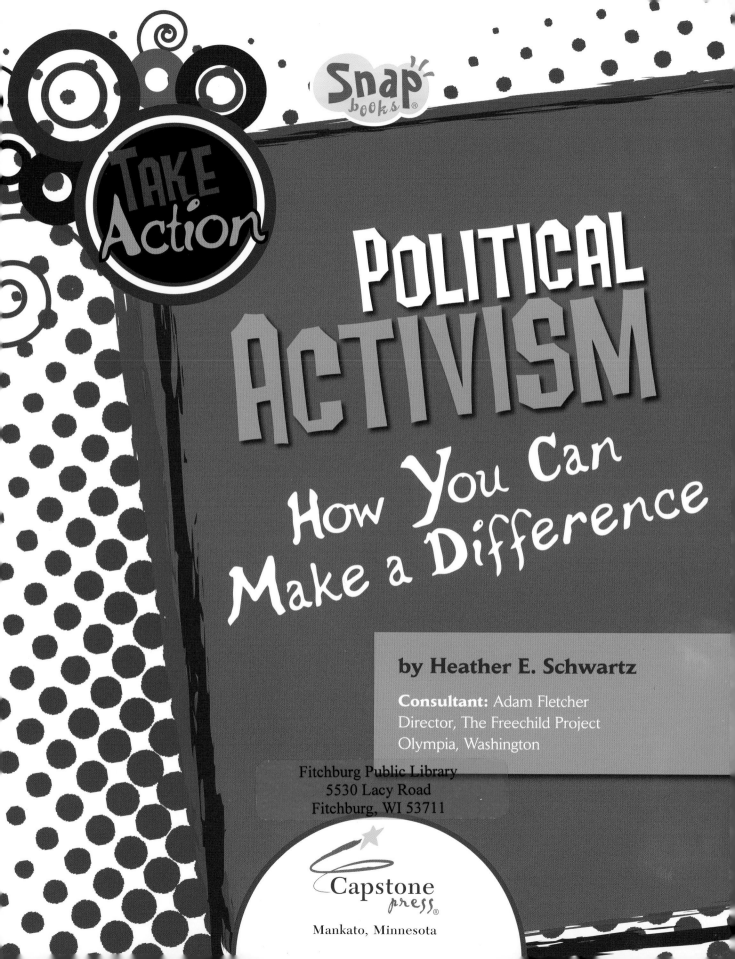

Snap books

Take Action

POLITICAL ACTIVISM

How You Can Make a Difference

by Heather E. Schwartz

Consultant: Adam Fletcher
Director, The Freechild Project
Olympia, Washington

CAPSTONE press

Mankato, Minnesota

Snap Books are published by Capstone Press,
151 Good Counsel Drive, P.O. Box 669, Mankato, Minnesota 56002.
www.capstonepress.com

Library of Congress Cataloging-in-Publication Data

Schwartz, Heather E.

    Political activism : how you can make a difference / by Heather E. Schwartz.

    p. cm. — (Snap books. Take action)

    Includes bibliographical references and index.

    Summary: "Describes what political activism is and serves as a guide explaining how youth can make a change
in their world" — Provided by publisher.

    ISBN-13: 978-1-4296-2799-3 (hardcover)

    ISBN-10: 1-4296-2799-9 (hardcover)

    1. Pressure groups — United States. 2. Political activists — United States. 3. Social advocacy — United States.
4. Social action — United States. I. Title. II. Series.

JK1118.S417 2009

322.40973 — dc22   2008026939

Editor: Jennifer Besel

Designer: Veronica Bianchini

Photo Researcher: Wanda Winch

Photo shoot scheduler: Marcy Morin

Photo Credits: All photos by Capstone Press/Karon Dubke, except:

Arianne Starnes, 21

Courtesy of Adam Fletcher, 32 (bottom)

Courtesy of Ben Smilowitz, 25

Courtesy of Katrina Sherwood, 17 (both)

Courtesy of Savannah Walters, www.pumpemup.org, 5, 6

Hot Shots Photo, 32 (top left)

Phil Riggan, 11

Essential content terms are **bold** and are defined at the bottom of the page where they first appear.

1 2 3 4 5 6 14 13 12 11 10 09

Table of Contents

CHAPTER 1

DRIVEN TO MAKE A DIFFERENCE

When Savannah Walters was 9 years old, she studied the Arctic. She fell in love with the beautiful animals and scenery there. Later Savannah learned the U.S. government planned to open the Arctic National Wildlife Refuge to oil drilling. She worried about how the drilling would affect the animals living there.

Savannah had talked to her mom about the problem. So when her mom met an activist who shared Savannah's concern, she got his name and number. Savannah called the activist. He told her Americans waste more than 4 million gallons of gas each day by driving on under-inflated tires. Savannah wondered why it was necessary to drill for more oil in a wildlife refuge. Couldn't people just inflate their tires properly to waste less?

Savannah also learned that gases from cars are the second leading cause of global warming. Now she had plenty of reasons to take action. If she could get people to properly inflate their tires, she might be able to help protect the Arctic Refuge. And she could help reduce global warming and slow the waste of gas at the same time.

But how could one kid possibly do all that?

Armed with information, a tire gauge, and passion, Savannah Walters decided to take action to save the Arctic National Wildlife Refuge.

Savannah started by asking her Brownie Girl Scout troop to help. Their goal was to make drivers aware of the problem. Together Savannah and her troop asked a company to donate tire gauges. Then the girls headed to a large parking lot. There they handed out the gauges to drivers. They also put flyers and balloons on the cars, encouraging drivers to pump up their tires. That was Savannah's first Pump 'Em Up event.

Since then, she's hosted many Pump 'Em Up events. She has also launched a Web site to help other kids host similar events. As her work gained attention, more companies started donating tire gauges. So far she has given away more than 10,000 free gauges.

Now, at age 16, Savannah is also working to change laws. As a political activist, Savannah has **lobbied** in Washington, D.C., to reach political leaders who make decisions. She's delivered speeches at the Capitol to promote proper tire inflation. She also spoke at a Senate rally. There she helped convince lawmakers to drop part of a bill that would have allowed drilling in the Arctic Refuge.

Savannah Walters

lobby — to try to persuade officials to vote a certain way

Savannah and her volunteers work hard to spread their message. They have learned that with hard work and dedication, young people can make a big difference in the world.

Now It's Your Turn

Activism means getting involved to change things for the better. Political activism takes that a step further. As a political activist, you work to create new rules or laws. You stand up to make your voice heard by people in power. That could mean talking to your coach or your congressperson. You could even become a leader yourself at school or in your community.

Many political activists start small. First they make change on a local level, in groups like a team, a class, or a community. Then, just like Savannah Walters, they build on their success. They create changes in their state, their country, or even the world. And so can you!

CHAPTER 2

WHAT'S THE PROBLEM?

STEP 1: BRAINSTORM PROBLEMS

How can you get involved, make change, and improve the world? Grab some paper and a pen, and take it step-by-step. The first step is pretty easy. Start by focusing on what you know best — your own life. Think of groups you belong to, like your school, your team, or your neighborhood. Is there anything you don't like about the way your soccer program is run? What would you like to change about your neighborhood? Think about your everyday activities, like riding the bus or practicing the violin. What would improve the activities you do each day? Could they be safer? Better for the environment? Less expensive? Pay attention to news stories about your community. Are you concerned about any of those issues?

Rule It Out

While you're brainstorming, consider rules that could be improved. Also write down any laws you want to make. Discuss your thoughts with friends, family, or teachers. Those conversations might spark even more ideas.

You don't have to figure out how to make any changes yet. Just consider what's important to you and what you want for your world. Write down all the problems and ideas you can imagine. Don't judge your ideas. Just write them down.

Tip Having trouble thinking up ideas? Take out a piece of paper and a pencil, and set a timer for five minutes. Then start writing down ideas that could improve your world. Don't stop to consider your thoughts. Keep your pencil moving until the time is up. This exercise is a good way to figure out what's on your mind.

STEP 2: BRAINSTORM IDEAS AND PICK A CAUSE

In step 1, major brainstorming brought up some problems. In step 2, you'll think of some ways you might solve those problems. For example, suppose you wrote down that your neighborhood has too much litter in the streets. Some goals might be:

- Organize a rally to clean up the litter.
- Change the law so anyone caught littering will be fined.
- Encourage citizens to vote for politicians who care about the issue.

List every possible goal that comes to mind. Don't worry about how you will reach the goals. Just get your ideas on paper.

Picking a Cause

Once you've done all the brainstorming, it's time to focus. Look over your list. Which idea do you care about the most? Be honest. You'll want to pick a cause you would be happy working on for weeks. Right now, you don't have to figure out how you're going to make change happen. You just have to figure out what you want to do. You can change your world, and it all starts with an idea.

Action Spotlight

In 1951, Barbara Johns lived in Prince Edward County, Virginia. At that time, Virginia and almost all southern states practiced segregation. That meant African Americans had to use different entrances to buildings and separate drinking fountains. Black and white students even went to different schools. And schools for African Americans were not in good condition. Barbara Johns' high school was overcrowded. Students didn't have enough books. But white students had plenty of supplies at their school. One day, 16-year-old Barbara decided to take action. She wanted a new school that was as good as the school for whites.

Barbara held a rally in the school auditorium. She spoke to the students about going on strike. In April 1951, 450 students walked out of the school. The students said they wouldn't go back until a new school was being built.

Barbara and her group also contacted the National Association for the Advancement of Colored People (NAACP). The NAACP had filed a lawsuit to fight school segregation. The NAACP used Barbara's strike in their lawsuit as proof that segregation needed to end. When the NAACP's lawsuit was settled, the U.S. Supreme Court ruled segregation in public schools was illegal. With Barbara's help, all African Americans won equality in education.

Statue of Barbara Johns, part of the Virginia Civil Rights Memorial

segregation — separating people because of their skin color

GET THE FACTS

STEP 3: **RESEARCH, RESEARCH, RESEARCH**

Taking action without good research is like jumping in the pool without knowing how to swim. Before you take action, make sure you understand all sides of the issue. In step 3, you'll become an expert on your issue. Find out how the problem started. What are other people doing about it? How would making a change affect others? Armed with knowledge, you'll be a stronger activist.

How Could Anyone Believe That?

There are always different opinions on an issue. Take the issue of a curfew for teens, for example. One person might believe a curfew would unfairly limit freedom for teens. Someone else might think it would keep teens safe. A third person might believe teens who are out late are likely to cause trouble. People base their beliefs on personal experience, values, and needs. You might disagree with someone, but opinions aren't right or wrong. Try to understand other ideas. Understanding other ideas will help you make a stronger case for your change.

Even people close to you, like your parents and your best friends, might feel differently about an issue. While that can be surprising and sometimes upsetting, all opinions deserve respect. Listen to what others have to say, and keep an open mind. It's all right to consider other perspectives and even change your views based on what you learn.

Ready, Set, Research

Research is important. But where do you start? You've heard this before, but the library is a treasure chest of information. Your local librarians can help you find books, articles, and even DVDs about your topic. Once you find those resources, devour them. Read or watch everything you can find. Take good notes about what you learn, so you can refer back to them later. And don't forget to jot down where the notes came from.

People Power

To get really complete research, you'll have to leave the library and talk to people. If your issue is local, go to town meetings. If you want a certain candidate elected, a campaign rally might be the place to go. As you're researching, you might also come across organizations that are working toward the same goal. Look those organizations up online. Check out their Web sites, and see what they are doing. Also see if you can find any contact information on those sites. Contact people within the organization and interview them about their work.

Experts are also a great resource. Experts have done a lot of research on specialized topics. They can give you another perspective on an issue. You might be surprised by what they can tell you.

Tip If you're a bit shy, try writing down your questions before your interview. Preparation will help you feel more relaxed.

Internet Info

Most research isn't complete until you've done some surfing. Web surfing, that is. You can find all kinds of information online. Look for scholarly articles, statistics, or even podcasts. Dig into the information you find. Learn about the background of your issue. Read about the laws that affect your cause. Find others who are working toward a similar goal. Get the facts you need to support your change. Remember to bookmark the great sites you find along the way.

Take It to the Top

Another avenue of research is talking to lawmakers. Don't hesitate to contact your class president, mayor, or senator. They might have other points of view you haven't thought of yet.

You can usually find officials' contact information online or in the phone book. Once you have their phone numbers, give them a call. You could interview them right on the phone, if they have time to talk to you. Otherwise, set up a time when you can talk in person. You can listen to the officials' points of view. And you can explain your ideas for change at the same time.

Question It

While researching, you'll probably find information that supports different ideas. Each side may be very convincing. Dramatic stories and statistics can be used to sway your point of view. It's a good idea to question all the information you get. Ask yourself these questions about the information you gather.

Is the information coming from a trusted **source**? Keep in mind that anyone can post things on the Internet. Check facts with other sources to make sure they're accurate.

Is the information based on stereotypes? If an article says, "All people with glasses are geniuses," you have to wonder if that's true. No one in any group is exactly the same. In fact, you probably know someone with glasses who is not a genius. Beware of sources that give such broad statements. And look to see where the authors got their information.

Does the information seem incomplete? Different perspectives should be represented in an article or Web site. If the information is one-sided, you aren't getting all the facts.

Tip Get organized. You'll make a better case for your cause if the information you need is ready when people ask. Collect Internet information in a folder on your computer. Keep written data in a separate notebook. Find a box for books, articles, maps, and other resources.

source — someone or something that provides information

Katrina Sherwood was 18 when she learned about plans for a megamall in her city. She was concerned the mall would create too much traffic. She also feared it would ruin agricultural land. Katrina decided to find out more so she could try to stop the project.

Katrina got to work. She talked to traffic and city planners to make sure the project was legal. She interviewed workers in a nearby city about how their town changed after similar malls were opened. Each time the developer filed documents about the project, she went to city hall for copies. She even called the developer with questions. She also studied maps to learn about the site where the mall might be built.

Katrina's research got her some attention. A newspaper reporter wrote an article about her. The article helped educate the community and gain support for her cause. The developer later decided not to build the megamall. Katrina's work played a part in that decision.

Katrina Sherwood

17

CHAPTER 4

PLAN OF ACTION

STEP 4: SET A GOAL AND MAKE A PLAN

You've chosen a cause, researched all sides of the issue, and given some thought to how you can make a difference. Now you're ready for Step 4 — mapping out a plan of action. Start by clearly defining your end goal. On a piece of paper, write down exactly what you want to achieve. Be specific. You'll be more likely to succeed if you know exactly what you want. If you want your city curfew to allow young people to stay out later, pick a time. When you fight for a 1 a.m. curfew, everyone will understand your goal.

Next you'll need to think about details. If you want to reach your goal, you'll need to set up a plan. Get specific when you're making a plan of action. Try to think of everything you might need to do or get. Be prepared for anything.

> **Tip** Don't be afraid to brainstorm big ideas. At the same time, be realistic about what you can do and how you can do it.

Here are some good questions to answer as you're
working on your plan:

- Who are the people you'll need to contact for help?
- What are you going to do? Will you be gathering signatures
  for a **petition**? Will you hold a rally? Will you run for
  school office?
- When are you going to do this, and how long will it take?
- Where are you going to do this? Will you need permission?
- Why are you taking this course of action over another?
  Why do you think this is the best way to achieve your goal?
- How? Plan your action step-by-step. Figure out the items
  you need or the advertising you'll do. Outline how many
  people you'll need to help you.

19

Consider the Risks

Before you act, make sure you understand what effects your actions might have. If you decide to lead a school strike, you could get in trouble. If you **picket** outside an organization, you could bother visitors. Also, picket lines often attract people who are against you. People may try to confront you and argue about your opinion. Or you could be arrested if you don't have the right permission to be there. Before you put your plan into action, think about the risks involved.

Some risks are worth taking for your cause. But if your ideas are meant to cause problems or hurt people, they'll backfire. Instead of supporting your cause, people will pull away. Ask yourself if the risks are worth taking in order to meet your goal. If your answer is no, consider another approach.

One Step at a Time

You don't have to overwhelm yourself and do everything at once. Major change starts with small efforts that grow. Remember Barbara Johns? When she started out, she only wanted a better school. But she became part of the fight for desegregation in public schools across America. Take it one step at a time, and you can make a big difference.

picket — to stand outside a place to spread your message

Sarah Boltuck would turn 18 in July 2008. That meant she would be able to vote in the presidential election in November. She also thought it meant she would be able to vote in the **primary** in February. For years, Maryland's law said 17-year-olds could vote in primaries if they turned 18 before the general election. But Sarah received a letter from her county Board of Elections. The letter said the state had changed the law. She would not be able to vote in Maryland's primary because she would not be 18 yet. Sarah didn't think that was fair.

So she took action. With her father's help, Sarah got in touch with a state senator. The senator took the case to Maryland's attorney general, who agreed with Sarah. The attorney general spoke with the election board, and the law was changed. Sarah helped 17-year-olds regain the right to vote in primaries.

Sarah Boltuck

Tip

Making change as a political activist takes team effort. Don't be afraid to ask for help.

primary — an election that chooses the party candidates

CHAPTER 5

TAKE ACTION!

STEP 5: PUT YOUR PLAN INTO ACTION

It's time to get out there and make your voice heard. How? Talk to people. Start with people you know, like family and friends. Make phone calls, send e-mails, or talk to them in person. Tell them about the issue and your ideas for change. Show your enthusiasm by explaining what you plan to do.

Once you have family and friends excited about your ideas, ask them if they'll help. When they agree, have a job ready for them to do. If you're running for class president, ask your sister to listen to your speech. If you're starting a petition, ask your friends to collect signatures.

Tip Always focus on the positive change you want to make. You'll come across as confident and optimistic. People will be more willing to support your cause.

Extend Your Efforts

With family and friends behind you, reach out to people you don't know. Step 5 is all about getting out there and working toward your goal. Create a Web site or hand out flyers. Speak at a town meeting to get your plan rolling. Meet with people in power who can change rules and laws. Help a candidate campaign for office. Or become a leader yourself. Whatever you decide, you're turning plans into action!

Tip Telling people about your cause can be scary, especially when they're people in power. Use notes or write a script, so you'll remember everything you want to say.

Action Spotlight

Ben Smilowitz was just 15 years old when he and two friends started the International Student Activism Alliance (ISAA). They started ISAA as a way to connect youth in political activism in their own schools, communities, and states. The group held meetings online. Students from all over the country met once a week to discuss strategies and take action. As president of the ISAA, Ben's own goal was to give students a voice in Connecticut's education system. Ben helped write a bill that would put two students on the State Board of Education. The bill was debated in the legislature. After more than a year, Ben's bill was passed into law. Two students now help the board make educational decisions every year.

Ben Smilowitz

legislature — the group of people who can make or change laws in a state or country

Small Steps Can Equal Big Change

It's not easy making change. Achieving your goal might take a long time. You might find that not everyone supports your cause. But be respectful of other opinions as you put your plans into action. You'll always win more support with a polite attitude.

And remember to stay positive. The law you fought against might pass anyway. Maybe you won't win the school election. But that doesn't mean your activism has to stop. If you're really dedicated to your cause, try a new approach. Talk to new people. And keep working toward your goal. Small successes now can lead to major change later. You might gain support from friends or get noticed in the news long before your work changes a law.

Political activism takes planning, hard work, and big dreams. It won't always be easy, but it will be worth it. Any action you take is a step in the right direction. You may not get the results you want right away, but making an effort is what it's all about. You can make a difference!

RESOURCES

There are hundreds of resources that can help you be a political activist. Below is a short list to help you get started in your research. But don't stop with this list. Find your own resources that will help you reach your goal.

Congress.org

Congress.org is a Web site that offers information about U.S. senators and representatives. The site includes contact information for elected officials, as well as the leaders' voting records. The site also allows users to post letters to officials or have their letters hand-delivered to Congress.

The Democratic Party

The Democratic Party promotes the election of Democratic candidates and works to promote the Democratic perspective. The party is based in Washington, D.C. There are also national, state, and local party organizations.

The Freechild Project

The Freechild Project is a program that provides tools, training, and advice to youth activists. The project's Web site offers information on a variety of issues and actions. There are many free resources and ideas for youth to use to work toward change in their worlds.

The National Youth Rights Association

The National Youth Rights Association is focused on the rights of young people in the United States. NYRA's mission is to empower youth by educating them about their rights and how to work with public officials. NYRA also has local chapters that work for change in communities.

The Republican National Committee

The Republican National Committee promotes the election of Republican candidates and promotes the Republican point of view. It is based in Washington, D.C. There are also national, state, and local Republican Party organizations.

Rock the Vote

Rock the Vote encourages young people to vote, run for office, and take action when they want to create change. The organization's Web site explains how elections are run, what your rights are as a student voter, and how to vote. Rock the Vote also has "street teams" to promote youth participation in the political process.

WireTap Magazine

WireTap is an online magazine for young people who want to create social change. The focus is on news and culture. Topics covered include politics, racial justice, war and peace, education, and the environment.

Youth Policy Action Center

The Youth Policy Action Center is a Web site that works to get youth involved in political activism. The site offers contact information for elected officials, election information, and ways to contact the media.

Glossary

brainstorm (BRAYN-storm) – to think of many ideas without judging them as good or bad

legislature (LEJ-iss-lay-chur) – a group of elected officials who have the power to make or change laws for a country or state

lobby (LOB-ee) – to try to persuade government officials to act or vote in a certain way

petition (puh-TISH-uhn) – a letter signed by many people asking leaders for a change

picket (PIK-it) – to stand outside a place to spread your message

primary (PRYE-mair-ee) – an election in which voters choose the party candidates who will run for office

segregation (seg-ruh-GAY-shuhn) – the act of keeping people or groups apart

source (SORSS) – someone or something that provides information

sway (SWAY) – to change or influence how someone thinks or acts

Read More

Botzakis, Stergios. *What's Your Source?: Questioning the News.* Media Literacy. Mankato, Minn.: Capstone Press, 2009.

Hoose, Phillip. *It's Our World, Too!: Young People Who Are Making a Difference: How They Do It – How YOU Can, Too!* New York: Farrar, Straus and Giroux, 2002.

Lewis, Barbara A. *The Teen Guide to Global Action: How to Connect with Others (Near and Far) to Create Social Change.* Minneapolis: Free Spirit, 2008.

Internet Sites

FactHound offers a safe, fun way to find educator-approved Internet sites related to this book.

Here's what you do:

1. Visit *www.facthound.com*

2. Choose your grade level.

3. Begin your search.

This book's ID number is 9781429627993.

FactHound will fetch the best sites for you!

Index

Meet the Author

Heather E. Schwartz is a freelance writer who writes mainly for children and teens. She has taught workshops for girls ages 9 to 14 and developed curriculum for Girls Inc. Part of the Girls Inc. mission is to inform policy-makers about girls' needs locally and nationally.

The political issues that concern Heather most include human rights, animal rights, and women and children living in poverty.

Meet the Consultant

Adam Fletcher is a private consultant who has worked with thousands of youth and adults, teaching them how to share their energy and wisdom with each other. He started The Freechild Project to share resources with kids on how to change the world. He also created SoundOut to teach people in schools how to listen to student voice.